AF492453

STILL YOU; THE REMINDER OF HIM.

A LOVE DRAMA.

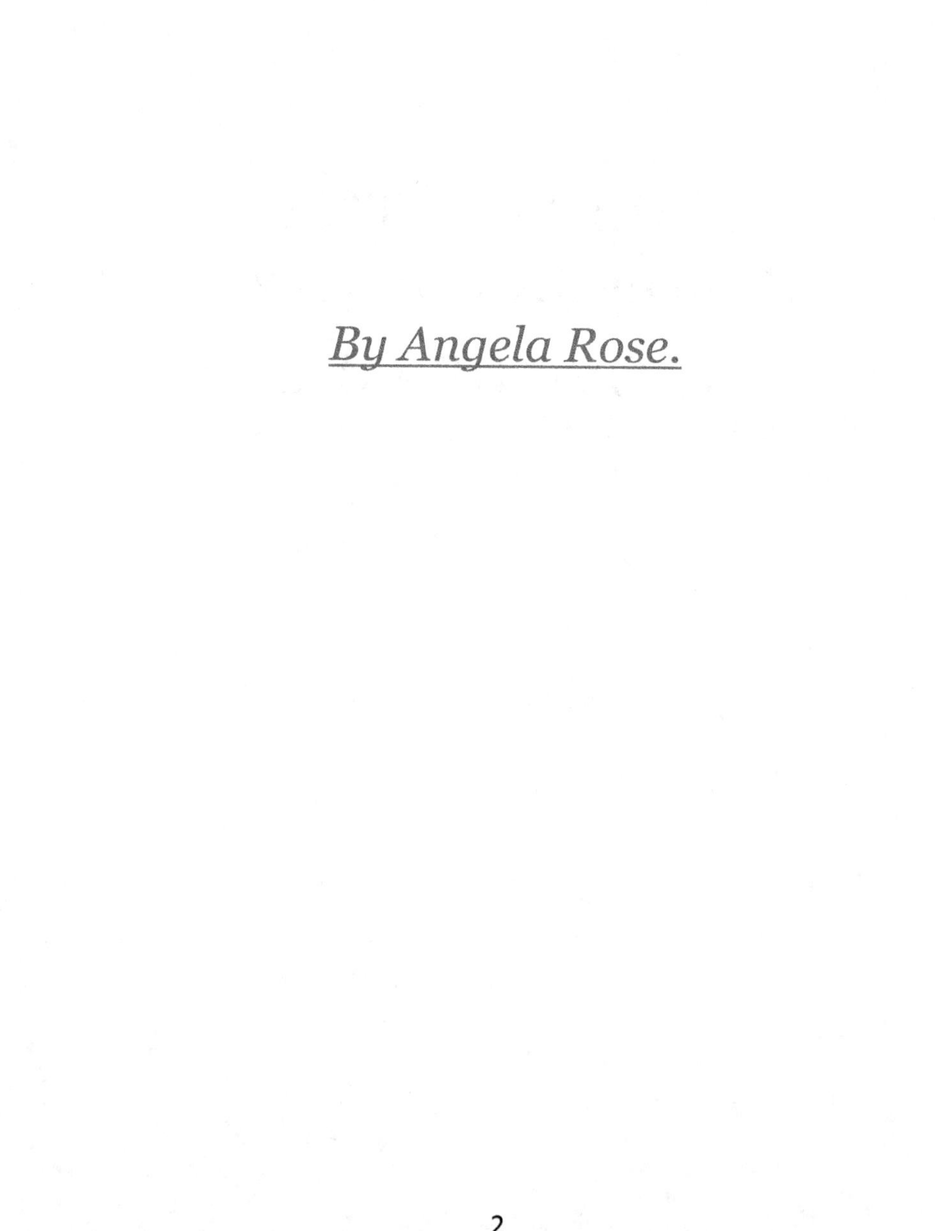

<u>*By Angela Rose.*</u>

copyright.

All right reserved. No part of this publication may be republished in any form or by any means, including scanning, photocopying, scanning, or otherwise prior written permission to the copyright holder.

copyright@ 2022 Angela Rose.

APPRECIATION/ACKNOWLEDGEMENT.

Special thanks to God for the privilege of being alive. Thanks to Mrs. Theresa for her support and inspirational words that have motivated me in so many areas of my life. I wish to use this medium to acknowledge and appreciate all those that have contributed in one way or the other in making this book a success. There are a bunch of names I couldn't mention; I want you all to know that I dedicate this book to you all.

Table of content

Chapter 1

Scene I

Betty locked herself up in her room the week. She refused to come out of her room, talk more of speaking to anyone. One morning Betty's door was just banging, it was as if the person locking wanted to break down the door by all means and bring her out of her room.

Betty: (with a cracking voice as if she has been crying all through the week) Go away I don't want to speak to anyone

Mr. Benson: (with a high tone) Hay young lady, you better come out of your room instead of locking yourself up over one stupid good-for-nothing boy. This is my house and since you are under my roof I won't have you separate yourself from the rest of the family just because you were heartbroken.

Betty: go away, I don't want to speak to anyone, if you want me to leave your house just tell me.

Mr. Benson: see young lady am losing it, am going to break this door now if you don't come.

Ruth, Betty's mom walked in, in the middle of the argument between father and daughter.

Ruth: (facing her husband, Mr. Benson) oh no dear please stop banging at her door. She is all grown up and has the right to come out of her room if she wishes or not, moreover, she is passing through a lot, she has been heartbroken and I feel it is our fault for not teaching her that these things do happens.

Mr. Benson: my dear I don't know what has over this girl, there are so many handsome men out there, why kill herself for one imbecile?

Ruth: dear just let me speak to her, I think with time she will come around.

Mr. Benson (as he makes the exist) you had better talk some senses into this your daughter's head. I don't know what she's thinking.

Ruth: (locking at Betty's door) come on baby, stop doing this yourself, that boy Steve or whatever his name is doesn't deserve you or your affections towards him, believe me when I say someone deserving of your love is coming, come on baby, please come out of your room. Am begging you.

Betty: mom please go away, Steve is my everything, I will come out when I feel like (as tears roll down her chicks).

Ruth: well I came here just to inform you that your best friend, Susan is here to see you, she came to speak to you about something, probably girls' talks, I know she knows your secret better than I do. Stop hurting yourself dear (as she leaves Betty's door to go get her friend).

Scene II

Susan, locking on Betty's door over and over again, it looks as if that door is not going to last for a long time due to the injuries inflicted on it by the locks and bangs it received almost every time for the past week. Finally, door the opens.

Susan: come on, look at what you have done to yourself, you look as if you haven't taken your bath for weeks now. Your room is all messed up.

Betty: not now please, if you are here to play the role of my mom and lecture me on what to do, you better leave.

Susan: (walked close to Betty and gave a tight hug) you know I care about you the most, you don't have to hurt yourself, while that bastard is out there enjoying himself despite what he did to you. Hay girl don't waste your tears over that fool. (as she leaves Betty who was feeling a little bit better seeing her best friend, then Susan picking and arranges Betty's room), don't worry girl I will help you tidy up the place, you just dash into the shower and take a nice bath. (as she hands Betty her towel)

Betty: thanks baby girl you are just an angel. (Betty made her way to the shower).

Susan: (gist with Betty as she is cleaning and Betty in the restroom), Betty did I tell you about the party happening this coming summer at Taxes in one of their old towns, common baby it goanna be an old school girl.

Betty: Susan you know am not interested in any party right now.

Susan: I know girl, but you don't have to hide in the shadows forever, who knows you might find a sweet cowboy. (Susan laughed).

Betty: am not interested in any relationship now, I don't think I will ever love anyone the way I loved Steve and he just broke my heart.

Susan: but Betty you never told me what transpired between you and Steve.

Betty: forget about it I don't want to talk about it.

 Betty came out of the shower some minutes later, by then Susan was done cleaning her room. Susan's phone rang.

Susan: (on a high tone) yes what do you want you fool? (She hang up) what rubbish.

Betty: Susan, hay girl you were rude on the phone, who was on the phone?

Susan: you won't believe who just called me.

Betty: who called you?

Susan: it was Steve, he has been calling me to reach out to you, since you guys broke up.

Betty: what did he say he wanted?

Susan: he said he wants to see you.

Betty: what for again?

As they were talking, the phone rang again.

Betty: pick the call and tell him that I said he should burn in hell; I don't want to ever see him.

Susan: (picked up her phone) what is it, I told you that she doesn't want to speak to you.

She hangs up again.

Betty: what did he say he wanted this time around?

Susan: he came to my house looking for me so that I can accompany him here to speak to you. I think he is on his way here,

Betty: how did he know that you are here?

Susan: maybe when he came over to my place my parent might have told him that am here.

Betty: he better doesn't come here.

Scene III

Mr. Benson and Ruth are in the living room, talking about how they will send their daughter, Betty to Santiago to stay a while with her auntie and a lock was heard on the door, a very handsome young man was locking the door. Mr. Benson went to get the door.

Mr. Benson: hello dear how may I help you?

Steve: sir my name is Steve, am here to see Betty.

Mr. Benson: (holding his jaws as he was thinking which Steve was this) Steve, Steve, are you the same Steve that broke my daughter's heart (with a high tone) what have you come here to do?

Mr. Benson: (calling out on Ruth, his wife) come and see what we have here.

Ruth: (as she walks towards the door) who is that dear?

Mr. Benson: a young man named Steve is here. He has come to check if Betty has taken poison, killed her herself for him since he is the only man left in the world

Steve: (mumbling words Mr. Benson cannot comprehend), sir I only came to, too!!!!!

Ruth: (as she walks in) you came to do what, after all, you had made my daughter pass through, you the effrontery to step your feet into my house again.

Mr. Benson: you mean he has been here before and no one told me?

Ruth: that was when they were both dating.

Mr. Benson: this is my first time seeing him, no one tells me anything about this anymore. Hay Steve or what are you called, this should be the last time I should see you in my house or anywhere close to my daughter again. Now get yourself out of my house.

As they talking Betty and Susan heard their voices from upstairs and decided to come down stirs.

When they heard their voice they already knew that it was Steve.

Betty: what the hell are doing here, I thought I told you not to look for me again.

Steve: please let me explain.

Susan: explain what Steve, this is not the right place to do that please leave Steve.

Steve: it's not what you think please, let me explain.

Mr. Benson: hay will you leave my house before I call the cops on you?

Betty: get out, you cheating bastard. To hell with your damn explanation.

Susan: just go. Get out of here Steve.

Steve left the house.

CHAPTER 2

Scene I

Immediately as Steve left Betty's house, everybody in the house was surprised and curious, they all wanted to know what actually happened between Betty and Steve and the reason why Betty refuse to let Steve explain himself. Questions started coming from left and right.

Mr. Benson: Betty, don't you think we need to know what happened between you and Steve? You locked yourself in your room for a whole week without saying anything.

Ruth: when he can you said get out you cheating bastard. What does that mean?

Susan: hay girl, I think you need to actually tell us what happened.

Mr. Benson and Ruth were surprised when Susan spoke.

Mr. Benson: Susan you mean you don't know between your friend and her so-called lover.

Ruth: Susan, she refused to tell you as well, I thought you both were a partner in crime.

Susan: she refused to tell me what actually happened.

Ruth: my dear please tell us what happened. Looking at Betty.

Betty: I have you guys, time without number that I don't want to talk about it. (as she walks upstairs back to her room)

Ruth: Susan please talk to your friend, try and find out the reason why she and Steve broke up.

Mr. Benson: something fishy is going on here.

Susan went back to meet her friend in her room.

Susan: hay Betty I know that whatever Steve must have done to you is hurting but I feel if you talk about it, it will let the pain go.

Betty: I think you have overstayed your welcome it is time to go.

Susan: are you sending me away

Betty: I told you and my parents that I don't want to talk about what happened between me and Steve, what happened with us is my business.

Susan: Okay fine whatever happened is your business and I promise never to ask you again, don't you ever tell me anything about Steve again. I don't want to hear how lovely he was, how you cannot get over him, and if you still want me to leave your house just say so one more time.

Betty: hay Susan, I don't mean to be rude but stop asking me about Steve. Please don't go away.

Susan: Okay, can we change the subject matter now?

Betty: you were telling me about one part happening this summer in Texas.

Susan: yeah girl, don't just tell me that you won't be there, it happens every summer and you have no choice but to come with me, I already got two tickets and you know whom the other ticket belongs to.

Betty: hmm okay I will give it try.

Susan: common girl, I feel is going to be fun, I have not been there but from what I heard I think it going to be fun. Maybe I might meet my prince charming there.

Betty: and he will be riding on a white horse, then he will say to you, Susan run away with me.

Susan: I will just say, oh my prince just take me away to your castle and do with me whatever you wish.

Betty: crazy girl you have watched lots of movies.

They both laughed Amid the laughter, Ruth walked in.

Ruth: hay girls, sorry for eavesdropping, I have been at the door for some time now, who is prince charming taking away?

Betty: mum, don't tell me you have been listening to us all this while. (Betty pointing to Susan) this drama queen here; wants a monster who she will be his beauty.

Susan: common girl, love is beautiful, just imagine me and my prince charming on the beach on our wedding day, me in my rose color or milk color dress and him in his royal attire.

Ruth: awn that will be beautiful, you girls just reminded me of when I first met your dad.

Both Susan and Betty laughed out loud.

Betty: common mum, we don't want to hear your old boring love story.

Susan: Betty if you don't want to hear, I want to, please ma tell me the first time you and Betty's dad met, am curious I want to know.

Ruth: I was a waitress working in a bar. You know as a young lady from a humble background, I need to work to support my family so picked up this job in a bar where I worked as a waitress. One Saturday evening Betty's father and his friends came to the bar. As they entered I saw Benson looking so handsome, tall, and well dressed. I couldn't stop myself from looking at his muscular body. When he was approaching me at the wine stands; as he drew near, my heart skipped and started beating very fast. He made his orders and I took his order to where they were sitting. After a while he called me, to ask for the bills, I handed him his bills and he asked for my home address and home number, I gave him and our love story started there; am happy it is ending well.

Susan: isn't that beautiful?

Betty: (laughing) old love, love in the bar.

Ruth: those were the days. I overheard you ladies talking about going to Texas for a party this summer.

Betty: yeah mom, Susan wants me to accompany her to the party.

Susan: yes, ma, the party happens every summer.

Ruth: as for me I will say you girls should go and have some fun but I don't know about Benson, what he will say after the last show Betty put up here last week.

Betty: mom am a big girl now, I decide when to talk and when not to talk to anyone moreover I have made up my mind, that this coming summer I will be in Texas.

Ruth: no one is saying that you are not a big girl but when challenges come learn to handle them like a big girl. You make sure you speak to your father before leaving this house.

Susan: sure as soon as we go downstairs will speak to Mr. Benson about our trip to Texas this summer.

Betty: I don't think that is necessary.

Ruth: it is very necessary; you have to speak to your father as you are under his roof; that shows respect.

Betty: I will soon leave this house for you guys.

Ruth: look at someone who could not handle a little heartbreak talking about leaving the house.

Betty: mom you don't understand how it feels.

Ruth: wow young so tell me how it feels since I was just born yesterday.

Susan: ma it is a promise from me we will speak to Mr. Benson.

Betty: mom I thought you were cooking something, am really hungry.

Ruth: yeah I made some salads, I don't know if you want some.

Betty: sure mom.

Susan: finally, someone agrees to eat something.

Betty: hay I cannot remember telling you that I have not been eating even as I was in my room, I had lots of snacks, and oftentimes when people were asleep, I do come down to eat something at night.

Ruth: I don't know why you decided to hurt yourself. (as she walks out leaving the girls behind)

Susan: baby girl when we go down to eat we will talk to your father about the trip.

Betty: I still don't think it is necessary.

Susan: it is girl, show some respect.

Betty: I have heard you, miss respect. When we go down to eat we will talk to him.

Scene III

At the dining table, Ruth is serving her husband his meal while the girls help themselves with theirs.

Mr. Benson: wow dear your meals always taste delicious. (as he eats the food faster)

Ruth: baby you know I got magic in my hands.

Betty: two love birds can we eat in peace?

Ruth: don't tell me you are jealous.

Mr. Benson: there is no chef in this whole world like your mother; I have not seen even one.

Betty: you are saying this to make her feel special.

Ruth: stop being jealous just wait till you get married so that your husband can complement you when you cook.

Susan: the food is delicious. I feel like eating the whole pot right now. (they all laughed)

Ruth: if you are done with this, you can always request for more.

Susan: okay ma.

Betty: (looking at Mr. Benson) dad we have something to tell you.

Mr. Benson: what is that dear?

Betty: dad, I and Susan will be going to Texas this summer.

Mr. Benson: what is happening in Texas this summer?

Ruth: they are having a get-together this summer in Texas.

Mr. Benson: so you are aware of it?

Ruth: yes, I overheard them talking about it and I asked them to speak to you about it.

Mr. Benson: what is this get-together all about?

Susan: it happens every summer, it is a get-together where young people like us come together to get to know ourselves and have fun.

Mr. Benson: I don't have a problem about you both going out this summer to anywhere you wish to go, where I will be crossed with you both is when what happened in this house last week repeats itself.

Susan: ok sir.

Betty: what happened last week is my business.

Ruth: common young lady keep your mouth shut. We wouldn't want what happened last week to repeat itself as your dad rightly said. How can a very beautiful lady like you lock yourself up because of one young man when there are numerous young men out there? The most annoying this about the whole incident is that none of us even knows what happened and you refused to talk about it.

Betty: mom that's the past that's the reason why I refused to talk about it. It has happened and I don't it I will do that for any man again.

Mr. Benson: you had better not. So when will you girls be leaving?

Susan: we will be leaving this Sunday sir.

Mr. Benson: whatever you girls need just let me know.

Betty: ok daddy am sorry if I was rude and thank you.

Susan: thank you, sir, it is getting late I will love to take my leave. Goodbye ma, goodbye sir am going home.

Ruth: hope you are satisfied.

Susan: yes, ma, thanks for the food, it was very delicious.

Ruth:(smiled) when you get home send my greetings to your parents.

Susan: ok ma, I will. Hay baby girl am going.

Betty: ok let me see you off

Mr. Benson: bye dear.

Susan; bye sir. (as she made her way to the exit).

CHAPTER 3

Scene I.

Its Sunday morning and Susan had already packed her bags and made her way to Betty's house. when she got to Betty's house; she saw her standing in front of the house waiting for her and the taxi they charted to take them to taxes.

Susan: (hugged her and they both exchanged pleasantries) hey baby girl you are already.

Betty: yeah I can't wait to leave this house (pointing at her house). what took you so long?

Susan: girl it was my mom, she delayed me; you know her always lecturing me on how to behave as if am still a kid.

Betty: our parents don't know that we are all grownups now.

Susan: what about the taxi driver?

Betty: his not yet here, I don't what could be holding him.

Susan: I think that him coming (pointing at an advancing taxi).

Betty: yeah that is him.

The taxi driver stops his taxi immediately after he got to the point the girls were standing; then came out of his car.

Taxi driver: oh ladies I presume you ladies are waiting for me. Am so sorry there was very huge traffic as I was coming.

Betty: you took so long.

Taxi driver: am sorry ladies, are these your bags; let me take them to the back of the car.

As the driver finished packing the bags. The ladies entered the vehicle and they started their journey to Texas. The journey from where they are living to Texas is a six-hour journey. They started their journey and in less than 5 hours they got to taxes. They arrived at Queens gust-in hotel where the girls will be lodging, as they drop;

 Susan: driver you were very fast.

Betty: the way you sped I feared for my life.

Susan: but that paid off, here we are girl.

Taxi driver: ladies that's the only way we could reach this early.

After a short friendly talk with the taxi driver, they went into the hotel, and by then the driver had already left. Queens gust-in hotel is a five-star hotel with very beautiful features; the hotel rooms were very beautiful and the hotel services were top-notch. Mr. Benson Betty's father was the one who booked the hotel for the girls. As the girls were handed the key to their room by the receptionist, they made their way to their room, freshen up, eat a five-star meal that they were served, and had a long rest. They slept for a long due to the long journey, by the time they woke up; it was already 11: 34pm.

In Queens gust-in hotel, every Sunday night is met for night parties. Usually, both gust in the hotel and gust outside the hotel always turn up for the parties. One of the reasons people usually gather is because the hotel is very close to the beach. When Susan and Betty woke up and decided to go outside. As they went outside they saw the party going on at various points within the hotel and the beach.

Susan: hay girl this place is beautiful as they say it is at night.

Betty: look at the beautiful designs and decorations

Susan: let go and join them, party girl.

Betty: you mean all these people lodge in this hotel?

Susan: no I don't think so. Girl what are we waiting for let's join them, I want to party. Wow!!

Scene II

As the girls were having fun at the party, Betty received a tap on her shoulder, as she turned she saw a Santiago; very tall and handsome.

Santiago: hay pretty, sorry if I may be distracting you from your dance, I saw you were dancing all alone. (stretching his hands) can I have a dance with you please?

Betty: I, you know hmm sure, sure we can dance.

As they were dancing to beautiful music played by the DJ.

Santiago: my name is Santiago. You look as if you are new in town.

Betty: yea I am, me and my friend Susan just came for the summer parties. My name is Betty.

Santiago: where are you from?

Betty: am from uptown. What about you?

Santiago: am from here, I feel maybe you ladies came to the summer party happening at the old valley hills.

Betty: yes, that's why we came, you know about the party.

Santiago: yeah I told you am from here; the party is the biggest of all parties happening this summer. People all over the globe do come from all asunder to attend the party. Believe me, when I tell you, it will be an experience that you will never forget.

Betty: let's hope it's worth the hyping.

Santiago: it worths it, till you come. It happening this Wednesday to Sunday. It is a memory that you will never forget.

As they were discussing and still dancing, they both exchanged phone numbers. Susan called out on Betty and asked her if they could both go in as it was already 2 am the next morning. As Susan walked in on Betty and Santiago.

Betty: hay Santiago meet my friend Susan and Susan meet Santiago.

Santiago: hello Susan.

Susan: hi.

Santiago: as your friend rightly said, am Santiago and you are welcome to Texas.

Susan: am Susan, it looks as if you are from here.

Santiago: sure am from here. Your friend told me that you ladies came to the biggest party happening this summer here in Texas. Have you been to the party before?

Susan: no a friend of mine told me about the party so I decided to come here with my friend Betty. This is our first time.

Santiago: it is a three-day party, believe the party will be your lifetime experience, after this summer, you girls will love to come back.

Susan: ok, am so sorry for interrupting your dance but I think it's really late, we need to go back to our hotel room.

Betty: yeah I think it is late.

Santiago: ok ladies, so Betty when next will I be seeing you?

Betty: I, I hmmm don't really know.

Santiago: What do you say maybe later this evening?

Betty: hmmm I, let's say....

Susan: yeah later this evening is ok, she will be there.

Betty: to where?

Susan: anywhere.

Santiago: you can come as well, Susan.

Susan held Betty by the hands as they ran off to their room. When they got to their room.

Susan: he is fucking cute.

Betty: yeah he is.

Susan: Are you thinking what am thinking girl?

Betty: hay naughty girl, what are thinking this time around?

Susan: maybe he is your prince charming. Did you see the looks in his eyes, when he was talking to you? Common girl, I think he likes you.

Betty: you have started with your telenovela again.

Susan: girl am serious that guy likes you. He even asked you for a date.

Betty: he didn't please, he asked both of us.

Susan: you know he did because he wanted me to feel among not that he really wanted me to come. I won't even be there.

Betty: why won't you be coming along this evening?

Susan: if am there, he won't be able to tell you what he wants to tell you.

Betty: so what will be your excuses for not coming?

Susan: I will think about it, then I will tell you what you will tell him. Let's catch some sleep, am tired, the party was lit girl. See you later (as she lies down to sleep)

Scene III

At about 2 pm later that Monday. Betty received a call from Santiago. Phone rang;

Betty: hello

Santiago: hello beautiful

Betty: hmm, who is this?

Santiago: so you don't recognize my voice?

Betty: no, please who is this?

Santiago: guess who I am.

Betty: you sound so familiar, just tell me who you are, am not good at guessing.

Santiago: ok, am the guy u met at the party last night.

Betty: hmm Santiago.

Santiago: how are you and your friend doing?

Betty: great, you.

Santiago: am good. I called to check up on you. So when will I see you later tonight.

Betty: I don't know; you decide am free.

Santiago: ok what about 8pm at your hotel, what do you think?

Betty: that will be fine by me.

Santiago: ok see you then. (as he hangs up)

Chapter 4

Scene I

Santiago sitting outside the hotel near the beach on a well decorated table waiting for Betty to arrive as earlier planned. He has already ordered Champaign, arranged a band, and decorated the table with beautiful rose flowers. All was set, the only thing stopping the dinner was the date who took too long to arrive as she was making up for her date. Finally, she arrives in her very beautiful dinner dark gown which was exposing the upper part of her boobs. As she approached Santiago stood up as a gentleman and ushered her in.

Santiago: you look very beautiful.

Betty: (smiled) thanks. This is really beautiful. You did all this. (looking at the decorations)

Santiago: common it is nothing. It is all for the beautiful princess sitting at the same time with me.

Betty: awn thanks it's beautiful but you shouldn't have done it.

Santiago: I will do that and more just for you. Soo, what can I get you? (as he opens the bottle of Champaign)

Santiago then signals the waiter to come to the table for their orders. As the waiter came he brought out a menu and they made their orders. It wasn't up to 5 minutes; the waiter came with their order. As they were eating Santiago kept staring at Betty and each time she noticed the stir she smells...

Santiago: you have a beautiful smile.

Betty: thanks. You are equally very handsome.

Santiago: stop that you are just pulling my legs.

Betty: am serious, u dope.

Santiago: (smiles) okay if you said so. You know the first moment I saw you at the party on Sunday night I knew you are the one.

Betty: hmmm the what?

Santiago: the one I have been waiting for all my life. Betty, I want you to be my girl (holding her hand) since that first day I can't stop thinking of you.

Betty: you see Santiago, for the past few weeks now I have gone through a lot.

Santiago: what happened?

Betty: I broke up with my boyfriend, don't even ask me what happened because I don't want to talk about it with anyone. The main reason why I came to Texas for the summer party is to clear my head and forget about what has happened.

Santiago: hay Betty I really get what you are saying but I want you to give me a chance. I have been single for some time now looking for the right person, as I saw you I had this conviction in my heart that you are the one heavens has prepared for me.

Betty: Santiago you are very funny. You know I just got to Texas, I need a little time to know you, just give little time please.

Santiago: you have all the time to think about it. So when will I see you again.

Betty: maybe on the Wednesday at the party.

Santiago. Oh yes, I will definitely be there. Hay don't miss the party. It is the biggest party happening this summer believe me.

After the dinner, Santiago walked Betty to her room at the hotel and they said their byes to each other with Santiago giving Betty a deep kiss which she did not refuse, hoping to see each other on Wednesday at the party.

Scene II.

Here comes the big day. A day Betty has been waiting for since they arrived in Texas. The summer party is going to last for good three days. On the first day at the Texas old town venue is already well decorated with beautiful designs, everyone was told to be in their cowboy and girl dresses as that was the dress code for the day. The event is like in the Mexican cowboy movies where they will be a live band, a lot of alcoholic drinks, and horses. At the venue....

Betty: oh min, Susan this place is awesome.

Susan: I told you, this is where prince charming is met.

Betty: naughty girl, you and this your prince charming of a thing, hope you find someone.

Susan: talking about someone, where is Santiago?

Betty: I think he should be around, when he called me at the hotel, he told me that he is already here. Susan tell me what you think of Santiago.

Susan: hmmm I think he is a nice guy. He is very handsome, tall, and masculine. wait, Betty hope is not am thinking.

Betty: what are you thinking now?

Susan: you are goanna accept his proposal tonight.

Betty: I don't know but...

Susan: but what, Steve is gone, he might be out there enjoying his life with other girls. Don't tell me you are still into Steve.

Betty: am so confused right now.

Susan: hay Steve is gone and gone for good. Move on, now look into my eyes and tell me that you will accept to be Santiago's girlfriend tonight.

Betty: (looking into Susan's eye) sure I will.

Susan: (hugging Betty) that my girl, I want you to forget about Steve. You refused to talk about what happened so forget about him.

As the girls were still discussing a voice came from behind.

Santiago: hello ladies.

Susan: hi Santiago, you are looking very handsome tonight.

Santiago: hmm thanks Susan, you ladies are looking so beautiful, sexy, juicy oh I don't have the exact words to express how you ladies look.

Betty: awn Santi thanks.

Susan: (wondering when Betty started calling Santiago, Santi) oh mine, Santi hmmm I better leave you both to talk. As she runs off.

Betty: naughty girl, what part of the venue are you rushing off to?

Susan: just around, see you.

Santiago: your friend is funny.

Betty: yeah she is. We have been friends since we were kids.

Santiago: wow that's a long time.

Betty: yup, she is so loving, she always gets my back. Common let's change the topic. I know that you are expecting a response from me concerning our discussion.

Santiago: hay Betty, I want you to believe me, if you give me a chance, I will make you the happiest woman on earth.

Betty: Santi I have given it a thought and mine.......

Betty turned, low and behold she saw Steve at the venue and she started stammering

Betty: I, I, I, hm, hm hm wanted to, to

Santiago: common girl what is the problem, why are you stammering?

Betty: am, am sorry (as she ran off towards the direction where Susan was enjoying herself).

Susan: what is the problem, why are you running?

Betty: he is still following me.

Susan: who.

Betty: turn around.

Susan: is that not Steve....

Scene III.

Steve approached the ladies. They all looked at each other very confused and Betty burst out...

Betty: why are you following me, I thought I told you that I don't want to see you again. What's your problem?

Steve: I didn't know that you girls will be here. It's just a coincidence.

Betty: coincident my foot, I know you, Steve. You will never learn till I call the corpse on you.

Steve: Betty, believe me, I didn't know that you will be here, I just came to have a good time.

Betty: yes, that's what you always do have a good time with your numerous girlfriends.

Steve: (burst out as well) what's your deal, how many times do I have to tell you that I don't have numerous girlfriends? You are the only girl I have ever been with, please believe me.

Betty: you liar, what about the girl I saw you with the other day making up in your room?

Susan: you did what, Steve?

Steve: that's not true Betty, you overheard sounds coming from my room when you came to my house. the sounds you heard were my friend Jonathan and your cousin's sister making out. You can ask them.

Betty: you see how easily you lie, how manage I ended up with you in the first place, that is the crazy question I kept on asking myself.

Steve: Betty please calm down let me explain what you thought you heard.

Susan: hay girl calm down, let's hear what he has to say.

Betty: okay Steve, go on feed us with your lies.

Steve: am not lying. Do you remember the other day I came to your house with my friend Jonathan, the day I met your mom and your cousin? Do you?

Betty: (no response)

Susan: please go on Steve.

Steve: that same day, Jonathan and your cousin exchanged contacts, I don't know how they ended up, all I know is that the day you came to my house it wasn't me that you heard, obviously you didn't see anything that day,

you only heard sounds and thought it was me,
I can swear with the sweet memories we
shared, Betty I have never and will never cheat
please stop this and believe me. I can't stop
loving you.

Susan: well you see Steve, even if that is what
happened Betty has moved on. Betty haven't
you?

Betty: (still no response)

Steve: I want to hear that from her.

Susan: hay baby girl tell him that it's over, tell
him that you have moved on.

Betty: (stammering) I, I huh hmmm never
knew that is what, I oh my God.

Susan: hay none of us can comprehend what
you are saying. Hay Betty say something.

       A familiar voice came from behind.

Santiago: say what (as he walked close to
Betty and gave he a kiss which is found
uncomfortable) what is happening here.
(looking at Steve)

Betty: hay Santiago, this is Steve, and Steve
this is Santiago.

They both exchanged pleasantries in an unwelcome manner.

Santiago: hay man.

Steve: hay buddy.

Santiago: you must be Steve, Betty's ex.

Steve: am Steve and you are?

Santiago: am Santiago Betty's new boyfriend.

Steve: she didn't make mention of you to me.

Santiago: does she? Do we need your permission for anything? (in a bit rising tone)

Steve: watch your tone man.

Santiago: and if I refuse.

Betty: you guys should please stop these. (as she ran off the scene)

Susan: the both of you should chill please (as she runs after her friend)

Santiago: you better go back to where you are coming from or else

Steve: or else what? (as they both depart).

Chapter 5

Scene I.

The next day, Betty was walking along the beach area when she heard Steve calling out to her.

Steve: hay Betty please wait.

Betty: what do you want Steve?

Steve: please I came so that we can talk.

Betty: talk about what.

Steve: talk about us, please.

Betty: there is nothing to talk about.

Steve: common Betty, stop doing this to yourself, yesterday am so sorry for what went down between me and that Santiago of a guy. Yesterday you didn't say anything I still have this strong feeling that you still have feelings for me, I want us to talk and after this conversation I promise never to bother you again if you say you don't want me anymore.

Betty: first before any discussion between you and me, how did you know that I am here and I was staying in this hotel?

Steve: I followed you yesterday when you ran off. I just needed to clear things up with you, I can't stand it seeing you with another person Betty, believe me, I have never cheated on you nor can I stop loving you. Please let's look for a quiet place to talk.

They both went under a tree to talk.

Steve: hay Betty I can still see the doubt in your eyes probably you don't believe me but I want you to call your cousin and ask her. I don't want you to call Jonathan, you might think he will lie to you but please call your cousin and ask her.

Betty: right now am confused.

Steve: is it because of that guy. (referring to Santiago)

Betty: that guy has a name. his name is Santiago, you know I barely know him but in the short time I have been with him, he sounds really nice.

Steve: hmmm okay, I still love you and will always, I came to explain myself to you and I cannot force you to reciprocate your love back to me, it is solely for me to choose.

Betty: I'm not gonna lie, I still love you, Steve. It's just that am confused.

Steve: Betty if I might suggest think about it tonight, then tomorrow you, I, and Santiago need to have a talk as grownups. Maybe then you decide either to be with me or Santiago.

Betty: Steve am sorry if I must have doubted you, I only thought you...

Steve: (cut in) you didn't allow me to explain myself.

Betty: am sorry. I want to go back to my room now.

Steve: Okay let me walk you back.

Betty: Sure

As they were heading to the hotel, they continued their discussion.

Steve: how did you get to hear about this place.

Betty: its Susan. What about you.

Steve: while I doing some researches online, I saw an ad that says the biggest summer party, pop up, so I applied, I never knew that I will see you here.

Betty: (smile)

Steve: why are you smiling?

Betty: no it's nothing.

When they got to the hotel they said their goodbyes and Steve gave her a kiss, the way she responded to the kiss simply shows she is very much in love with Steve.

Steve: bye see you tomorrow then.

Betty: bye.

Scene II.

As Betty and Steve were still discussing, Santiago came to the hotel's room where Betty and Susan lodged. A knock on the door was heard.

Susan: whose there?

Santiago: it is I Santiago.

Susan: oh Santiago common in. (as she opens the door)

Santiago: how are you doing Susan?

Susan: am doing great, you?

Santiago: well am okay. What about Betty.

Susan: she went for a walk at the beach area. Please make yourself comfortable.

Santiago: (as he sits) sure, when is she going to come back?

Susan: I don't know, she said she needed to walk in order to clear her mind.

Santiago: hay Susan I want you to tell me the honest truth, do you think Betty is still in love with that guy Steve or what is name again.

Susan: you see Santiago, Steve is Betty's first love and you know how it usually is with our first love. I don't really know what is going on her mind but I feel you should first speak to her, then give her time to think.

Santiago: (looking straight into Susan's eye and lost in thought)

Susan: Santiago, Santiago!!

Santiago: hay Susan sorry please continue what were you saying.

Susan: I'm done talking, what the matter? What are you thinking?

Santiago: no nothing much, I was just lost in thought. So tell me more about yourself, you don't someone or what, sorry for asking doe just that I haven't seen with anyone.

Susan: well I have been single for some time now, the guy I once dated left without a word or a call.

Santiago: since when?

Susan: for about two years now.

Santiago: sorry some guys don't really know what they want. You see Susan you are very beautiful no much worries someone special out there will come your way someday. (as he was discussing with Susan, he was still lost in thought) she should have been the one I would have seen first instead of chasing clouds he said to himself.

Susan: are you sure you are okay? I notice you are thinking about something.

Santiago: no, no am good, I was just thinking about something. It is just a minor thing.

Susan: we fruit juice in the fridge, hope you won't mind?

Santiago: sure I don't.

Susan then stood up from where she was sitting to go get fruit juice for Santiago. As she was pouring the juice, they still continued their discussion.

Susan: I just hope you will like it. I know most country guys like you prefers hot drinks like whiskey Johnny walk and the rest.

Santiago: yes, I love hot liquor but at times I do take juice when there is none liquor around like now.

Susan: those kind of drinks are usually hot.

Santiago: they help to keep me warm inside you know.

Susan: I only take those when we are at club or outings. (as she hands Santiago a cup of juice)

Santiago: thanks you are very caring.

Susan: thanks.

Santiago: you know my family is from Mexico, they migrated to Texas some years back doe I was born here so taking hot drinks is like the family's tradition.

Susan: how long have your parent stayed in Texas.

Santiago: over 35 years now. I and all my siblings were born here.

Susan: wow.

Santiago: oh my I totally forgot I had something I was doing please when Betty comes tell her I came by.

Susan: okay I will.

Santiago: bye.

Susan: sure bye.

Scene III

As Steve and Betty were saying their goodbyes, Santiago came out of the hotel's entrance and met them kissing.

Santiago: what the hell?

Betty: oh mine, hay Santi please calm down, let me explain, Steve was just leaving.

Santiago: you should have told me instead of wasting my time. I never knew you were back with this fool.

Steve: hay you better watch it or else.

Santiago: what will you do.

Betty: please guys not here.

Santiago: all you should have done was at least call me and tell me you didn't wanted me; that you are back with this thing (pointing at Steve)

Betty: Santi please stop call him names.

Santiago: I will call him whatever name I wish.

Steve: you know Betty am only keeping my cool because of you.

Betty: (on a high tone shouting at the top of her voice) Santiago I have not still accepted your proposal and I don't think I will, I still love Steve and I hope you to understand. I am so sorry if I might have got your hopes up. I don't think I can live without Steve please try to understand. I and Steve wanted having a discussion with you concerning it, we never thought that you will show up today.

Santiago: but this bastard cheated on you.

Steve: I didn't cheat on her, I have never and will never.

Santiago: what the hell is happening here.

Steve: you see man I want you to calm done, let talk like grownups please.

Betty: I don't think that is necessary today please let do that another day please.

Santiago: I can't believe this (as he leaves).

Betty: Steve I want you to go as well tomorrow we will talk; I have had enough of today.

Chapter 6

Scene I

Susan's phone rang three days after Santiago came to the hotel.

Susan: yeah hello, Santiago where have you been.

Santiago: hello Susan. How are you doing?

Susan: am great, we haven't seen you for the past three days. Where have you been.

Santiago: I been around, what of Betty, how is she doing?

Susan: she is great.

Santiago: is she there?

Susan: no she went out with Steve, you know they are back together.

Santiago: yeah, well that is not why I am calling you. Am outside the hotel, please come out.

Susan: where?

Santiago: outside please come out.

Susan: okay am coming out.

About ten minutes after their call Susan came out to meet Santiago.

Santiago: hay Susan how are you doing.

Susan: good I thought you just left without goodbyes.

Santiago: I didn't leave, after what had happened between me and Betty with that guy Steve I just decide to lay low you know.

Susan: yeah, sorry man I don't think anything can separate Betty from Steve. I told you before Steve is Betty's first love, they have been together since kids.

Santiago: wow, they called and told me they wanted to see me so that we can talk but I didn't show up, I hope we can rearrange and meet once again.

Susan: yeah you guys really need to talk like adults you know.

Santiago: yeah but that's not why am here.

Susan: okay so why are you here?

Santiago: I actually came to see you.

Susan: me.

Santiago: yeah Susan.

Susan: for what?

Santiago: I don't know how this sounds but Susan since that day at the hotel I haven't stopped thinking of you. I tried keeping it to myself but I can't, coupled with the incident with Betty but I can't stop thinking of you Susan.

Susan: (stammering) hmmm Santiago I don't know what to say. I don't know how this will sound to Betty if she hears it.

Santiago: I and Betty are not together and I strongly feel God used what transpired between I and Betty to bring you to me. If it is talking to Betty, I will speak to her myself and I feel she will not have problems with that. Hay Susan It is not about Betty now, it is about you and I (holding Susan by her hands) I want you to please accept me and I will make you the happiest woman on earth.

Susan: I don't know what to say now. I think you should speak to Betty and thrash it out even if you guys did not work out I still feel guys need to talk, then you can come back to me.

Santiago: I will call Betty and arrange for a meeting for all of us to talk. Susan the day I was in the hotel room with you was the day I realize that you and I are meant to be please don't say no.

Susan: I can only give you my response after we might have met and talk things through.

Santiago: I will arrange for the meeting tomorrow.

Susan: okay till then.

Santiago: hope you guys are not leaving Texas anytime soon.

Susan: we were planning to leave by the weekend.

Santiago: okay there is still a little time.

Susan: huh yeah.

Santiago: okay see you tomorrow.

Susan: yeah

After their discussion, they said their goodbyes. As Susan was about going in. Santiago just really needed to confirm if Susan feels anything for him. He held her by the waist and gave her a deep kiss and she responded passionately to the kiss which confirmed to Santiago that she also had feelings for him.

Scene II

In the evening of the next day, they all gathered at the hotels reception as earlier planned by Santiago.

Santiago: I noticed that we are all quite, first of all I want to start by saying a big thank you to you guys for honoring my invitation and I want to apologize for not turning up when you guys once called me for this meeting.

Betty: hay Santi we are not angry with you, I actually thought you left Texas for a while since we didn't hear anything from you.

Steve: I understand how you feel man; I just want you to know that I bear no grudge man (as he stretches his hands for a handshake)

Santiago: (responded to the shake which signifies that there is no more beef between them) sure man, hope we are all good.

Betty: sure.

Steve: is it just me or something is wrong.

Betty: how babe.

Steve: (facing Susan) hay Susan you are not saying anything. What happened to the girl that usually light up every party?

They all laughed...

Susan: am good maybe it because of the weather, it's a bit cool.

Betty: yeah the weather cool.

Santiago hmmm yeah a bit, please before we go further with the long talk and laughter, I have not still stated the main reason for this gathering. (sounding serious)

Steve: which is.

Santiago: I and Susan are going out, I don't know if those are the right word, I made my intensions doe she has not accepted till I speak to you guys first.

Steve: wow I think that a great news.

Betty: wow hay Susan, is that why you are silent all this while, common girl, you know I and Santiago are not dating and it will really make me happy to see the both of you together.

Santiago: hay Susan, please I want you to accept my proposal as your boyfriend (as he holds her hands and looked straight into her eyes)

Betty: what the hell are you waiting for girl.

Steve: say yes, say yes.

Betty: common accept to be his girlfriend girl, say yes, say yes.

Susan: (holding Santiago's hand) yes I love.

Betty: huh hmmm love is in the air.

Santiago: I promise to make you the happiest woman on earth. Love you too.

Steve: wow is this love, is this love that am feeling (singing)

Betty: hmmm my baby can sing.

Steve: you know am gifted baby.

Santiago: that reminds me when will you guys be going back.

Steve: bro we should be out here by Saturday.

Betty: do you feel like coming with us.

Santiago: I hmmm am thinking let me see how things work out before Saturday.

Susan: since I don't really have much to do at home I think I will stay for a while.

Betty: hmmm

Susan: what?

Betty: naughty girl.

Susan: I just wanted us to spend some time you know.

Betty: I know but I know you the more hahaha.

Susan: ha-ha you try to be funny right.

Steve: yeah I think it will be a great idea the both of them staying together you know, to get to know themselves will be great.

Santiago: (looking at Susan) yeah babe you want to stay?

Susan: yeah.

Santiago: I would have love to go guy but you know work.

Susan: I understand, that why I goanna stay back.

Santiago: that baby it was God that bring you to me.

Betty: huh.

Steve: Betty come let go, let leave them to talk.

Betty and Steve left Santiago and Susan to talk and have the rest of the night for themselves.

Santiago and his new found love went to his home while the old love birds went back to their hotel.

Scene III.

Saturday morning Betty and Steve has packed their bags, Santiago and Susan came and took them to the railway station. Before the train took off...

Susan: I goanna miss you guys.

Betty: same.

Steve: so when are we goanna see again?

Susan: am goanna stay here for a little long time.

Santiago: before winter we will see each other again but we will always keep in touch on the phone.

Steve: yeah sure.

Susan: I think the train is about to leave.

Betty: yeah I can see people going into the train, common girl give me a big hug.

The girls hugged themselves so tight as if they were never going to see each other again.

Steve: common baby let us, bye guys.

Santiago: bye my man.

Betty: Susan hope you have spoken to your mom.

Susan: sure I did.

Betty and Steve left, while Susan remained in Texas to spend quality time with Santiago.

THE END.

www.ingramcontent.com/pod-product-compliance
Lightning Source LLC
Chambersburg PA
CBHW072122150726

47999CB00005B/2086